I0214087

HARVESTING THE MOON

POETRY BY
DEBORAH K. TASH
WHITE WOLF WOMAN

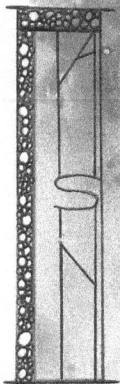

A Fumbled Book Press Original

Published by:

FBP

Fumbled Book Press
Oakland, CA

Copyright © 2020 by Deborah K. Tash

In Her Image Studio

All rights reserved. Without limiting rights under copyright reserved above, no part of this book may be reproduced, stored or introduced into a retrieval system, or transmitted, in any form or by any means (electronic, mechanical, photocopying, recording or otherwise), without the prior written permission of both the copyright owner and the publisher.

ISBN: 978-0-9987640-4-7

First Edition: 15OCT2020

Joan and David Lincer, Publishers

Fumbled Book Press brings titles that we know and love back from "Out of Print". Each title is reset with care in Adobe InDesign.

Catalog: www.FumbledBookPress.com

Other Titles From

Deborah K. Tash
White Wolf Woman

Inspired By The Tides

Voice Of The Poet In Troubled Times

Soft Power/Reclaiming The Sacred Cunt Project

Illuminated Poems

Ravens At My Window, Ravens On My Roof, Roses On My Table

108 Dreams Of A Night Poet

Journal Sketches And Hidden Voices

120 Sextets

and coming soon:

*The Gods In The Mirror/An Erotic Adventure Tale Of Spiritual
Transformation*

Contents

Acknowledgement

If not for the friendship and encouragement of Norma and Elaine, both of whom taught me the poetry of the body in the midst of the adversity, deep loss and challenge of the early 2000s, I would not have finally been willing to put my words out into the world in this book.

INTRODUCTION

I started writing poetry at eight years old as a way to survive an abusive and turbulent childhood. As a survivor both of incest, sexual and physical abuse and years of surgery and hospitalization due to polio, I was a solitary child. My poetry was a form of salvation and has been shaped by my early childhood experiences as I navigated a path to healing and transformation. It took me many years before I had the confidence to share my work with anyone.

This selection of poems was originally compiled as a chapbook for the Finishing Line Press' 2009 New Women's Voices Chapbook Competition. It has been expanded to include several more poems, which were not included for that competition, as well as the background drawing, Moonlight Impression.

HARVESTING THE MOON

POETRY BY
DEBORAH K. TASH
WHITE WOLF WOMAN

Harvesting The Moon

Walking down a darkened street as
Moonlight illuminates memory
I find my need to write
As if it were part of my flesh

A skin of loneliness
Longing for the touch of night
Searching for the syllables
That will open pleasure's arms

Literal descriptions opening wounds
That fester without air
I dig beneath the reality of atoms
To find the place of soul

Tearing the viscous membrane
The sticky fiber of cultural consensus
Away from the true body of being
That waits quivering with anticipation

I do not want to write about suffering
When all that breathes is animated by desire
Encompassing that tangle of skin with
The unknowable limits of mastery

Moonlight more clearly defines
Than midday's stark openness
That sweet dark fruit
That trembles and falls from the tree of life

22 SEP 05

Embracing The Perilous

How does one embrace the perilous
The journey to the depth
Where the ocean is no longer blue
Death waiting in the shape of a dolphin

How does one embrace the perilous
Collecting stones from the bottom
To build an altar
For the temple of the Self

How does one embrace the perilous
When the body holds clues
Like a tangle of tumor vessels
At the base of the skull

How does one embrace the perilous
Stepping off the cliff gently
Into an unknown horizon
To find an interior knowledge

How does one embrace the perilous
When the tunnel sheds no light
Leaving no way back
To the season of the familiar

How does one embrace the perilous
As the questions become the answers
Dreams suffusing daylight
With the colors of the soul

For Elaine

18 DEC 06

For Norma

What use is there
    in constant chatter

Naming the connection
    in an overbearing
    desperation

To make it real

When all it requires…
    hands
    hearts
    eyes

That look into
    each other

Come with us
    Each day

Hooray!

18 DEC 06

Spirit Of The Creek/Incanto

When you hear the music of nature
Singing in your blood
Filling you with the essence of water
Filling you with the essence of stones
Then the spirit of the creek
Is calling you

Calling to your deepest memories
To the rich vein of reality
That waits for you in the center of your self
From a place that hides nothing
In ancient tongues of joy and reverence
An incanto for your soul

07 OCT 08

Shaman In An Urban Landscape

I am a place complete
All of my parts held firmly
With the hub of the crow's wings
'Til conversation becomes the norm

The little one behind the wall
No longer fears the dark
The giant's leg outgrown
No need for cupboards now

Now that the warrior's song
Has become a familiar tune
A place of standing firm
Opens all the shuttered windows

Integration marks this place
Where once the separate parts
Fought tooth and nail
To remain in hidden corners

The High Priestess is my hand
Moving the pen without hesitation
Holding the warrior to account
For the gifts the Spirit brings

Ancient memories stain the sunlight
When the crows fly overhead
Their raucous cry demanding attention
To the details of ancestral offerings

The little one behind the wall
Steps out into the throng
No longer the thrall of fear
Her power joins with the warrior's

Her golden hair reflects the light of the stars
The sun at its closest orb
Informs her new awakening and
She is a child of knowledge

The knowledge of an inner power
No separation of the mind
As the Guardians at the Gate
Welcome me into the landscape of fulfilled desire

The boundaries of my being
Open into the place of singing trees
Where the language of the birds
Is not lost in the dull city streets

Attuned now to the dialog between
The concrete and the wind
My heart seeks magic
In the colors of my dreams

17 MAR 08

The Paradox Of Stones

Steady and stable
       or
Cold and bruising

A foundation for love
       or
Its painful undoing

Built of stone
       or
Stoned to death

13 AUG 05

Grinding The Bones

Grinding the bones of betrayal
To a fine ash of memory
I make a paste with the sweat
That looks from the struggle
To find meaning
Hoping to bind my heart's
Scattered pieces and
Release the stones

13 AUG 05

Ticking

The clocks tick in staggered unison
Each room settled in its own timepiece
A harmony of watchfulness
Waiting to be tucked away
Like a small forbidden secret

Too long uncovered
It creases in the light of day
A chancre of loneliness and despair
Just a coating of dust below the surface
Poised on the edge of dissolution

Like a certain kind of poetry
Subtle and more about the labyrinth
Then the arena of late night programming
Ready to burst into fine mist
To be reabsorbed in the deep silence

That harmony suggests an unresolved
Conflict snared in the gears of memory
Grinding the fine mesh of cooperation
To a fabric of terror and immobility
Staining the future with half-truths

Until even the gentle ticking becomes forlorn
Resolution obscured by the colors of fear
Indecision the counterpoint
To a pattern of withdrawal
Sitting on the edge and waiting for renewal

13 AUG 05

A Room For Desire

My closet door stands open
The spill of possessions
Tangible made manifest
Abundance and the incalculable
A universe of YES
For years of desire

I rest beside the textures
The colors filling my dreams
Looking for a deeper acceptance
For a physical form
To shape my path through life
Hoping for beauty

Surrounded by the beautiful
Images of Eros and Circe
The triune Goddess and
Her twinkling forest angels
Remind me of my own inherent
Oneness with the Divine

The candles flicker
Lighting up a room filled
Altars to pleasure and sensuality
Mounds of sweater and cloth
To delight a lover's eyes
While dawn lights the sky

26 DEC 08

Strength Of The Heart

How to shape the words to fit
When a certain catch of temperament
Could harden into a heart of stone
A barrier to fend off the grip of fear

It is simply that to push away
The ugly, addicted and insane
Is the reaction of a frightened child
Trapped in a family of origin

Would it be a tithe due hell
To smile at the red faced horrors
Locating a graciousness inside
For the ones who resemble a brother

Or is it just that resemblance
That makes the street people
Feel like the threat of loss of self
Knowing how close they've come

Clear it with the pendulum of knowing
Finding the words that heal
So simple to the trained
With the strength of the heart

31 DEC 08

After

I want it to be small
A furry burrowing thought
So light you could
Put it in your pocket
Take it with you
When you go
Just enough weight
To remind you
Familiar and warm
That you are loved

13 DEC 08

Poem #1

The city no longer sleeps
The purr and hum of its morning
Gives backdrop meaning
To my solitary reverie

You are not here just now
Though you called
Wanting contact yesterday
Your sweet voice rough with longing

Yes, I heard it and
When I retrieved your pictures
From the camera chip
I saw it in your eyes

The "call of the wild" you said
A raven perched on top of shelves
Mysteries of desire beckoning
And we are held in its embrace

08 DEC 08

Poem #2

In an unexpected hour
The cold burnishes the dark
Year after year the cycles turn
Still leaving the unknowable

In the wake of what could be
The moments of confidence dwindle
Or swell with renewed hope
Dependent on the imagination

In every singular heart
The rhythms of life express
A constant symphony unheard
Except in the moments of connection

In that moment when eyes meet
To plumb the depths of another's soul
All competition is left behind
In the deep embrace of Spirit

09 DEC 08

I Am Shy Tonight

I am shy tonight
At the thought of you
Because it has rooted
I am reluctant to speak

Would that I could
Make my words
Sing with the melody
Of your eyes

That would be poetry
Indeed

26 FEB 01

Another Morning Dawn

Singing in the morning light
Small territorial voicings
Trill and thrill in green knowing
City songs groan
Droning in counterpoint as
The bus labors up the hill

A neighbor hammers on a wall
But the birds, undaunted
Find the trees good companions
As they fill the sky with melody
Blessing the roots in the ground
Earthing life even as they fly

16 MAY 05

I Laughed 'Til I Reached My Door

New part of town
Dogpatch at the foot of the hill
Warm wind and bright sunlight
Etch the deserted street
Outlining the industrial landscape
As I walk alone

Stewing in creative juices
Dormant memories of lovemaking
Just begin their summer thaw
I watch a single car
Creeping along the patched pavement
Not noticing the abundant parking

Walking towards it
The car's inexorable progress
A slow surprise
Magnetizing my speculation
One driver and a passenger
With her head in his lap

Her hair obscured her mouth
As his look of ecstasy
Brought the wet alive
Drenching the cloth between my legs
Remembering my own pleasure
I laughed 'til I reached my door

06 AUG 05

The Reset Button III

Only an echo of your essence
Eating in this chicken and pasta palace
How many times did we eat here

My ninety-three year old friend
Teeters on the brink between the worlds
While you are gone ahead
All counsel about her death
Useless in the face of yours

All the little things we'll never do
Pile up in the corner
A snowdrift in a hot summer sun

I've stopped waking up in the dark
Shocked to know that a tree limb
Was the answer to all your desperation
While I've come up for air
Forty-nine days a week past

The scrim of grief boils away
So that I can think of you again
Rejoicing in how you touched my heart

09 JUN 08

19

A Table By The Window

A blimp glides by in the slipstream
The distant trees cheering it on
As birds fly formation outside the window
Not unlike the day I watched you
Walk across the lazy twilight street
To join me here

My heart ached all week
With an unsustainable decision
Your face an underscore
Of its impossibility
As you crossed the quiet street
To join me here

Tonight the twinkling lights
Pretend that snowflakes have fallen
As dusk descends beyond the glass
While somewhere in my dark city
You cross a street in time, but not
To join me here

09 DEC 08

Poem #7

The city rests in misty grey
Wind and rain calmed
Drops linger on glass
The year is coming to an
Anxious close

The green lens shifts
Perspective in the growing
Consciousness of a new age
No amount of popular ridicule
Can forestall it

Though there is only a little
Understanding increases
Enough that now a man
With a brilliant mind and
Chocolate skin has won

The eternal grinding of
Skin to dust
Dust to earth
Is witnessed by the ancients
Rock, tree, river

They pause not at all
Except for humanity's carelessness
Still the tides turn
The moon rises and
Love remains constant

14 DEC 08

Stepfather

Dreaming of an old voice
Just beyond my bedroom door
A combination of present and
An entirely terrifying past

When I had no recourse
Too young to know how to say it
With no one to protect me but
My own stubborn "disrespect"

That word meant nothing to me
Because for years I used it
A stand in for the right to
Dominion over my own life

A way to keep his hands off me
Once I understood their meaning
His voice in the dark
An exposure unwelcomed

A violation of trust and body
On the early morning landing
When all I wanted was the comfort
That every child deserves

18 DEC 08

Smoke And Ash

Such hot fires
Burning away the impulse
Instincts for safety
Captured in the flash
Of passion's white hot eye

So much seduction
Washed through his voice
Hooking them with his charm
Promises of heat and hunger
As if they were true

To reach out for it
Was the final mistake
All that seemed once
Made from flame alone
Only smoke and ash

24 DEC 08

After Meditation

When the body has released
Long held fears that bear
A fruit of intolerance and disgust

When ugliness is no longer
A terror of sameness and deceit
Mirroring internal unworthiness

When the smooth skinned beauty
Is seen as nothing more
Than an option of nature's design

26 DEC 08

Just So

Dark on dark
Richness on my tongue
The smeared thick texture
Of your liquid sex
Mixed with the sweetness
That only a jungle of taste conveys

Is it the memory of chocolate
That makes my cunt throb
The single lush delicacy
You brought for dessert
Licked off my nipples
With a playful tenderness

The two are intertwining
Each time you speak my language
Bring me a truffle delight
Light fires in my imagination
Wash the dishes after dinner
Lick my ear with your voice on the phone

With all the multiple pleasures
Of your hard insistence
Banging against me
Even as you sleep
'Til I can not contain my own desire
And words of love spill out

My liquid center exposed
Where you've sucked away the shell
The weight of water
That is your emotional proof
Both flow together in the dark
Like chocolate on our tongues

19 DEC 08

Poem #5

I thought I'd write a political poem
They're all the rage
At poetry slams and
There's no end to death, injustice and cruelty

I could work up a righteous indignation
Condemn and rant and blame
Point my finger and shout "Shame! Shame!"
To nods of agreement and approval

All the corruption recently come to light
Could fuel a bonfire of disdain
Riots and protests and revolutions
Fill more than just one page

But all that said changes not a thing
Does nothing to anchor the angel nature
Deep into the wilder dark places
That stain the human soul

Illumination is not borne by politics
The steady slow drum beat of change
Is more akin to the rhythms of the blood
The dance of hope and love

This is a long prelude
To the memory of your vulnerable eyes
Alight with pleasure
Awakened in the night of a full moon

Small revolutions like journeys
The turning of the Wheel
Lifetime to lifetime
Seeking a deeper kinship with the Divine

That Tantric chant of renewal
Inherent in every conscious act of lovemaking
Leads us inward to the source
Where the soul's liberation waits in the Light

Calling on the gods
Invoking the Feminine Divine
Re-membering the Christos
All acts that heal the world

Let me be a poet of the soul
Though better said, a poetess
Let my orgasms call the angelic hosts
To witness their transformation

Let me be a conduit of words and images
That anchors the angel into the animal
To be as fully human
As intended in the plan of the Divine

And join me, if you desire...

12 DEC 08

Don't Take the "-ESS" Away From Me

Don't take the "ess" away from me
Poetess is what I claim
I am no poet
Truncated without my femaleness

But all that I choose
I express through my sexual nature
And the soft warm moisture
Of the mysterious womb of birth within me

Call me hostess then, and
Actress, priestess
And celebrate with me the "ess"
For I reclaim it as my own

29 MAR 02

Envy

Perhaps the envy
Is shaped more like
The first development

Before the chromosomes
Respond to chemical desire
Changing the clitoris
Elongating and pulling it
'Til it no longer nestles
Safely inside the body
Exposing the ovaries
To the hazards of weather and
Hard knocks
As they descend

Perhaps the envy
Extends to the brain
Which loses volume and mass
As the x gains ascendancy
Losing touch with
The sisterhood of life
Androgens causing
Separation from the original comfort
Maybe the envy is
More than just a longing

To return to the womb
-You throw like a girl-
Don't you just wish

26 APR 07

Not A Guy

I am not a guy
I have breasts
Cup size D
My cunt swells with desire
       yes
         I reclaim that word!
Not a prick
I am also most definitely
Not a dude

Here we are
       sitting
The restaurant is full
Two of us and
"How are you guys tonight?"
Both us women
At this table
Not a male in sight

The ones who look like girls
Stare in hypnotized
Cultural conformity
Puzzled
       Huh?
When I point out that
I am not a guy and
Especially not a dude

The males who are guys
Are belligerent
      dismissive
      angry
Rudeness their response
To my request
To be named
Unwilling to grant me
My feminine due

How did it happen
After years of hard work for
      womanhood
That these younger ones
Are willing to conform
To a male cultural imperative
      duuuude
Don't call me that
Because I am not a guy

27 APR 07

Poem #6

Mist
The first caress of rain
Obscured the distant ocean
As just we two stood on the hill

The city lights glistened
A crescendo after the sun
In warmed moisture rich air
Mist

13 DEC 08

Deborah K. Tash
White Wolf Woman
In Her Image Studio
inherimage@artlover.com
www.inherimagestudio.com

Photographs:
Donnie Felton/Almac Camera
M. Joseph Schaller, PhD
Deborah K. Tash

Deborah Karen Tash, White Wolf Woman, a Shamanic Artist, poet and healer, is currently Artist In Residence for herchurch and curator of ARISE GALLERY in San Francisco, California.

Creating as a spiritual practice and means of self-expression has been the foundation of her work both as a visual artist and poet. She combines both whimsy and Shamanic influence on the path of beauty in her art.

Working in series she allows idea, inspiration and dreams to guide her in the choices she makes determining the kinds of medium and techniques to employ for each piece.

She works with painting, mixed media, sculpture, mask, drawing, fiber, collage and clay often weaving them together in a single multimedia expression.

Deborah continues to explore how to use symbol and image in order to uncover the shape and influence of transformation on her interior life and that of the viewer, as well.

www.ingramcontent.com/pod-product-compliance
Lightning Source LLC
Chambersburg PA
CBHW061955090426
42811CB00006B/940

9 780998 764047